Close Your Mouth

Buteyko Clinic handbook for perfect health

PATRICK MCKEOWN

Buteyko Books

Dublin Cork Limerick Galway Sligo Athlone

Close Your Mouth

First published in 2004 by: Buteyko Books an imprint of Asthma Care Ireland
Unit Six, Calbro House, Tuam Road, Galway, Ireland

Web: www.buteykoclinic.com
Email: info@buteyko.ie
Tel: 00 353 91 756229

© Patrick McKeown 2004
Cover Design and illustrations by Global Solutions of
www.globalsolutionsindia.com
Typesetting by iSupply
ISBN: 0-9545996-1-6
A CIP catalogue record for this book is available from the British
Library.

The therapeutic procedures in this book are based on the
training, experience and research of the author. The
information contained in this book is not intended to serve as a
replacement for professional medical advice. This book teaches
the importance of breathing through the nose, how to practise
simple breathing exercises and adopt lifestyle guidelines
aimed at promoting good health. Do not change or alter
medications without the consent of a registered physician. The
author and the publisher specifically disclaim any and all
liability arising directly or indirectly from the use or
application of any information contained in this book.

A wise person ought to realise that health is their most valuable possession.

Hippocrates

Contents

Chapter 1

Elixir of Life

Take a breath now, and think about it carefully. Breathing is the elixir of life. More than that, breathing is life. We humans can live without water for days and without food for weeks, but we cannot live without air for more than a few minutes. Think about how we Westerners view food and water: we know that the quantity and quality of food and water we consume determines our state of health. We know that having too little means starvation or dehydration, and that too much leads to obesity and other health problems.

Breathing is the elixir of life

Why then does the quantity and quality of our breathing receive so little attention?

Surely breathing, which is so immediately essential to life, must meet certain conditions? Why have other cultures, particularly in the Eastern world, recognised the importance of correct breathing to health for thousands of years, when we clearly don't?

A new dawn is emerging by recognising that correct breathing volume is fundamental to maintaining good health. This new beginning is based on the life's work of Russian scientist, Professor Konstantin Buteyko. The Buteyko (Bhew-tae-ko) Method is recognised by the Russian medical authorities. Not alone that, but it has been backed up by two independent scientific trials held in the Western world. The method has received widespread attention including a detailed debate in the UK House of Commons in July 2001. Evidence from thousands of people worldwide - who improved their lives forever by applying Buteyko breathing exercises - is also available. All persons can learn it and use it; the method is very simple, will entail minimum disruption to your life, and you will notice an improvement to your health in as little as seven days.

Correct breathing volume is essential to perfect health

The Discovery

Over four decades, Russian scientist Professor Konstantin Buteyko completed pioneering work on illnesses that develop as a result of breathing more air than the body needs. His life's vocation provided humanity with what is arguably the greatest discovery to date in the field of medicine.

As a medical student, he discovered from his observations of hundreds of patients that their breathing was closely related to the extent of their illnesses. The greater the volume of air inhaled by a patient, the worse the sickness, he noted. This newly-discovered relationship between breathing and health was so precise that he was even able to predict accurately the exact time sick patients would pass away.

Professor Buteyko

The greater the volume of air inhaled, the poorer the health

In April 1980, following trials in Leningrad and at the First Moscow Institute of Pediatric Diseases, the Buteyko Clinic Method was officially acknowledged as having a one hundred per cent success rate. This research was directed by the Soviet Ministry's Committee for Science and Technology. Over two hundred medical professionals teach this therapy at present from centres located in major towns throughout Russia. In addition, the basic model of Buteyko's theory forms part of University medical curriculum.

Buteyko's discovery on October 7th, 1952 has improved the health and saved the lives of many thousands of people. Now that his discovery is becoming better known in the Western world, it will save the lives of many more.

Breathing and Health

The volume of air we inhale and exhale is measured in litres, and measurements are usually taken over one minute.

The standard volume of normal breathing for a healthy person is three to five litres of air per minute.

If we breathe more than our body needs, it is known as hyperventilation. If this is happening on a day-to-day basis, it is called chronic hyperventilation.

Severe overbreathing can be fatal if it is sustained over a short period of time, so it is plausible to accept that there will be negative health effects caused by less severe but still excessive breathing over a long period of time.

Buteyko's discovery is that long-term overbreathing leads to the build-up of organ damage, resulting in the development of illnesses specific to the hereditary traits of each person.

Often, overbreathing is not obvious or noticeable and therefore was called 'hidden hyperventilation' by Professor Buteyko. Other researchers, such as Robert Fried in his book *Hyperventilation Syndrome*, have agreed with this description. Obvious indicators of a person who hyperventilates are: sighing regularly, sniffing, upper chest breathing, yawning, taking large breaths before speaking and, of course, breathing through the mouth.

Symptoms of overbreathing

Hyperventilation contributes to many conditions, but **because it receives very little attention in the diagnoses of illnesses,** many patients suffering from various physical symptoms sometimes spend years going from doctor to doctor looking for the cause. This group of patients are often labelled as 'psychosomatic' and there is a belief that the condition is 'all in the head'.

Physician Claude Lum noted that hyperventilation "presents a collection of bizarre and often apparently unrelated symptoms, **which may affect any part of the body, any organ and any system".**

Some of the symptoms of hyperventilation affect:

The respiratory system in the form of blocked nose, wheezing, breathlessness, coughing, chest tightness, frequent yawning and snoring.

The nervous system in the form of a light-headed feeling, poor concentration, numbness, sweating, dizziness, vertigo, tingling of hands and feet, faintness, trembling and headache.

The heart; typically a racing heartbeat, pain in the chest region, and a skipping or irregular heartbeat.

The mind, including some degrees of anxiety, tension, depression, apprehension and stress.

Other general symptoms include mouth dryness, fatigue, bad dreams, nightmares, dry itchy skin, sweaty palms, increased urination such as bed wetting or regular visits to the bathroom during the night, diarrhoea, constipation, general weakness and chronic exhaustion.

Your respiratory system

Your respiratory system consists of the parts of your body used for the delivery of oxygen from the atmosphere to your cells and tissues, and for transporting the carbon dioxide produced in your tissues back into the atmosphere. If cells and tissues are to function properly - if you are to live - your body needs the atmosphere's oxygen. Your nose, mouth, pharynx, larynx, trachea, bronchi and lungs are all part of your respiratory system.

Carbon dioxide is produced as an end product of the process of breaking down the fats and carbohydrates that you eat, and this gas is brought by your venous blood vessels to your lungs where the excess is exhaled. **Correct breathing results in the required amount of carbon dioxide being retained in your lungs.**

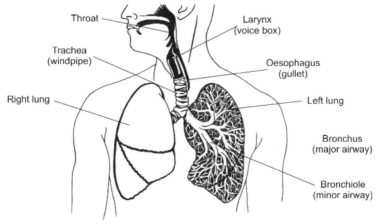

Our Lungs

Cause and Effect

The sustenance of life requires oxygen and carbon dioxide. Just as excess oxygen results in damage to the lungs when the toxicity level is higher than antioxidants can counteract, too little carbon dioxide impairs the correct functioning of all organs.

The key to Buteyko theory is that carbon dioxide is not just a waste gas; it is essential for all metabolic functions.

Dr. Yandell Henderson put it well when he wrote: *"carbon dioxide is produced by every tissue and probably acts on every organ,"* in the Cyclopedia of Medicine published in 1940. Medical science has long recognised that the required amount of carbon dioxide in the little air sacs of the lungs, the alveoli, for a healthy person is five per cent. This is well illustrated in any university medical textbook. However, constant overbreathing leads to a loss of carbon dioxide and the concentration may drop as low as three-and-a-half per cent. Butekyo found that a level of below three per cent led to death.

How does overbreathing affect carbon dioxide?

If you breathe in a large volume of air then you will breathe out a large volume. Humans don't inhale air to store it in any form in the body, so therefore the volume exhaled has to be the same as the volume inhaled. The more air we inhale causes more air to be exhaled, and this greater quantity of exhaled air results in too much carbon dioxide being carried out of the body.

**Large volume of air in =
Large volume of air out
This causes a loss of carbon dioxide**

Overbreathing is a bad habit

Breathing more than your body needs over a period of hours, weeks, months, or years will result in the day-to-day levels of carbon dioxide remaining low. Our respiratory centre becomes accustomed to or fixed at this lower level of carbon dioxide and determines it to be 'correct'. Our respiratory centre will therefore instruct us to overbreathe to maintain this low level of carbon dioxide, even though the rest of the body's organs and tissues are suffering. In essence it is a bad habit.

Why is carbon dioxide so important?

Here are two of the more important reasons why carbon dioxide is essential to human life:

- **Transportation of oxygen**

Oxygen is relatively insoluble in blood, so ninety-eight per cent of the gas is carried by haemoglobin molecule. The release of oxygen from haemoglobin is dependent on the quantity of carbon dioxide in our alveoli/arterial blood. If the level of carbon dioxide is not at the required level of five per cent, oxygen "sticks" to haemoglobin and so is not released to tissues and organs.

This bond was named after the physician who

discovered it and is now known as the Bohr Effect.

Breathing too much results in our organs receiving less oxygen.

Have you ever noticed that you get dizzy from taking big breaths?

- **Dilation of blood vessels and airways**

Carbon dioxide dilates the smooth muscle around airways, arteries and capillaries. Following an increase in carbon dioxide, there is greater distribution of blood due to dilation of blood vessels. Instant feedback comes in the form of reduced symptoms and increased body warmth due to improved blood circulation. People with respiratory problems experience a dilation of their airways and so can breathe better.

Correct breathing improves blood flow and helps open our airways

Why do we overbreathe?

Earlier on I explained that when we overbreathe on a permanent basis, the respiratory centre in our brain is trained to accept a lower level of carbon dioxide. This level is determined to be correct even though it is less than the body requires for good health.

There are many reasons why we overbreathe but not all of them may apply to each individual. The following six factors are more prevalent in countries of increasing modernisation and affluence, and this helps explain why diseases of civilisation are so prevalent in the same countries.

1. Diet

Over-eating increases breathing because the body requires more energy to digest and process food. Instead of listening to the body and eating when hungry, as we have done for thousands of years, society now dictates at what time we should eat. In addition, we condition ourselves to eat more food than is necessary. How many times have you continued to eat all the food on your plate, or all the courses on offer, even though you didn't feel hungry?

We have lost the art of listening to the body about what it needs. People in ancient times only ate when they were hungry. The primary reason for this was that hunting and gathering food required effort, and that more energy had to be spent to gather a larger quantity of food. Our ancestors didn't have the luxury of accessible modern-day convenience stores, supermarkets and fast-food outlets to obtain something to eat whenever they desired, so they ate less and better food.

Protein, especially animal protein, and processed foods contribute to overbreathing. Professor Buteyko believes that food is the single biggest contributor to overbreathing. A supplementary factor is the use of chemicals and pesticides in growing all foodstuffs. The body has to work harder to remove the increased amount of toxins in food. This increases breathing.

2. Misconception of deep breathing

The traditional view in the Western world is that deep breathing is conducive to fitness and maintaining good health. A 'deep breath' is misinterpreted as a 'big breath'. This fixed belief prevails among sports coaches, schools, hospitals, asthma clinics, radio, TV, magazines and even Western yoga. The most common instruction to those taking exercise or experiencing stress is to 'take a deep breath'. By exercising in the gym or taking a walk along the beach, you can see how many people believe in the benefits of big breathing.

In the Eastern world, reduced breathing and breath control is very much enshrined in culture and philosophy. Its therapeutic value has been recognised for centuries.

3. Stress

Interpreting outside events, often those over which we can have no control, results in stress. Stress can be positive in the form of laughter, for example, or negative in the form of anxiety. Breathing is increased by stress, and in turn breathing leads to excitability of many brain areas, resulting in states of anxiety, panic and many psychological problems. At this point, one factor will feed off the other thus maintaining a constant state of arousal.

4. Temperature

Living in a hot and stuffy environment causes overbreathing. While body temperature is primarily controlled by skin pores and sweat glands, wearing too much clothing causes us to revert to primitive mouth panting as a way of regulating temperature.

Thanks to central heating and PVC windows and doors, our homes are better insulated and are becoming progressively warmer. Years ago houses were less well insulated and cooler, and a draught often brought fresh air through gaps under doors or between window frames. Research has demonstrated that mild or cool environments assist reduced breathing.

5. Lack of physical exercise

Exercise enables the body to accumulate large amounts of carbon dioxide produced by metabolic activity; lack of physical motion means less activity and less carbon dioxide.

For most people now, work means more mental effort and less physical activity. Even most of our forms of entertainment take place indoors, such as cinemas, theatres, computer games and satellite television. Out of an average twenty-four hour day, eight are spent sleeping, fourteen sitting and just two hours standing or walking. Compare this to the average day of our ancestors who spent all their waking hours completing tasks that demanded physical activity.

6. Over-sleeping

Professor Buteyko's research shows that lying down horizontally for a long period of time causes severe overbreathing. Most deaths occur between the hours of 3.00 and 5.00 a.m. when the body's level of carbon dioxide passes below its lower threshold due to excessive breathing during sleep. Professor Buteyko emphasised that the position which causes the most overbreathing is sleeping while lying on one's back. Incidentally, this can be observed among many people who stop snoring when they are turned over onto their side.

"One needs to eat less, breathe less, sleep less and physically work harder to the sweat of one's brow because this is good. This is a fundamental change, this is true restructuring. This is what we need to do these days."

Professor Buteyko

Chapter 2

How Is Your Breathing?

"Habit is either the best of servants or the worst of masters."

Nathaniel Emmons

Breathing is the most important physiological function you can exercise control over and this is something that can easily be achieved through increased attention, observation and will-power.

Benefits of reduced breathing;

Reduced breathing due to what is called the Bohr effect leads to better oxygenation of all of the body's cells and tissues which in turn enables all the organs to function more efficiently. Almost everyone who has attended the Buteyko clinic in Ireland has reported increased energy levels; less dependence on stimulants such as caffeine; increased calmness and concentration; reduced anxiety and normalisation of weight - all within a relatively short period of time.

Chronic complaints such as wheezing, coughing, blocked nose, headaches, constipation and spasmodic conditions - caused by incorrect breathing and dietary factors were also gradually eliminated.

Basic breath retraining

There are three basic steps towards breaking the habit of overbreathing;

● **Step One**

Become very aware of your breathing. Feel, watch and listen to your breathing as much as you can during the day, paying particular attention to what causes you to take big breaths.

Ask yourself some questions. Is your breathing a still, silent activity or does it involve large inhalations and body movements?

Observe other people who are perhaps breathing with their mouths open, panting when shopping, or at bus stops; it is also possible to notice a person's breathing characteristics over the telephone. Even though all of these people may seem to enjoy good health, many of those who have bad breathing actions may already have or are likely to develop health problems in the future.

● **Step Two**

Learn to breathe through your nose. Breathing through your nose at all times is the correct and only way to breathe.

Some people seem to spend most their lives with a blocked nose and many have tried, without success, every nasal spray and therapy on the market. In this book those very people will be taught an effective exercise for unblocking the nose in a matter of minutes. This will be the first step on the road to permanent and comfortable nasal breathing.

• Step Three

Application of Buteyko Clinic Method to reverse chronic hyperventilation. When asked for a simple definition of his theory, Professor Buteyko said it is this: the reduction of the depth of breathing by the relaxation of the respiratory muscles to create a little air shortage. Two words he directed at his patients were "breathe less". This is the very essence of Buteyko breathing. Through the Buteyko Clinic Method the individual learns to breathe in a **calm, silent** and **still** manner.

"The perfect man breathes as if he does not breathe"

Sixth century B.C. philosopher Lao Tzu

How to interpret breathing diagrams

A diagram illustrating breathing patterns will accompany many of the exercises. The following symbols are used for each diagram. Refer to this diagram periodically in order to understand those that follow.

Taking a Breath in

Letting a Breath out

Holding the Breath

How to interpret breathing instructions

Nasal Breathing For Health

The nose has a number of features designed to bring cold dry outside air to a more acceptable condition before it enters the lungs. The mouth, however, is not intended to condition atmospheric air - it is merely for talking, eating and drinking.

• Our nose **warms** the inhaled air far more effectively than drawing it in through the mouth.

• Air is **filtered** to prevent pollen, dust and bacteria from entering the lungs. On any one day, a person may inhale from 10,000 to 20,000 litres of air laden with foreign particles. Whereas the nose can remove these deposited particles within fifteen minutes, it takes **60-120 days** for them to be removed from the small air sacs (alveolus) within the lungs.

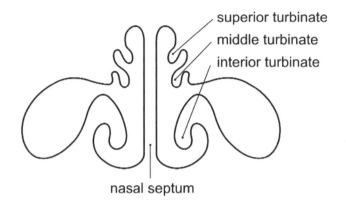

Frontal view of interior of the nose

• **Lungs require a warm moist** environment and therefore it is imperative that the air drawn into the lungs meets this condition. The nose humidifies inhaled air by increasing moisture content.

• It is just as important to **breathe out through the nose** as it is to breathe in through it, despite a common conviction, particularly among sporting professionals, to the contrary. By breathing out through the nose, part of the moisture contained in the exhaled air is retained, thus reducing moisture loss. Breathing out through the mouth results in a greater loss of carbon dioxide and may lead to dehydration. This can be observed by breathing onto a pane of glass and then checking the residue of moisture left.

• Nasal breathing helps to regulate volume. All mouth breathers overbreathe and as a result suffer some symptoms of hyperventilation. The nose is a smaller channel to breathe through, and therefore it helps to reduce the volume of air as there is about fifty percent more resistance. It is possible to overbreathe through the nose but to a lesser extent.

A partially blocked nose is common with nasal breathing, one nostril will be partially blocked while the other is free to work. Check to see which of your nostrils is blocked by placing your finger over one nostril and breathing through the other; then repeat using the other nostril.

You will find that after three or four hours the blocked nostril will usually clear and the previously clear nostril will become blocked. This is a natural pattern which enables one nostril to rest at a time.

• Mouth breathing results in irregular and erratic breathing while switching to nasal breathing brings more rhythm to the process.

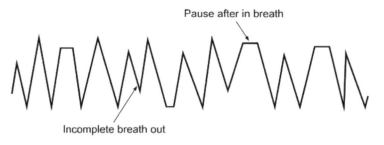

Pause after in breath

Incomplete breath out

Erratic & irregular mouth breathing

The importance of breathing through the nose tends to receive very little attention from the medical profession. It seems to be accepted without question that some people will breathe through the mouth and others through the nose. However, breathing through the mouth is detrimental to your health and this is emphasised to all patients who learn breath retraining.

Mouth breathers have generally poorer health and may go through life with an uncomfortable and permanently blocked nose. Furthermore, mouth breathers have a higher incidence of cavities and gum disease than those who breathe through their nose.[1]

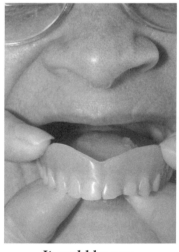

It could be you

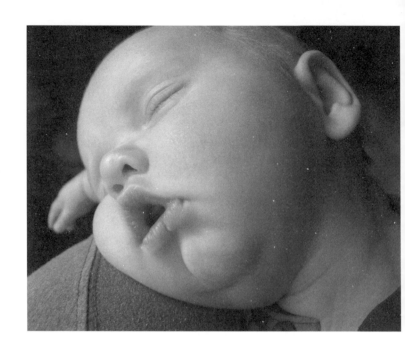

Baby could have an even better start to life

It was observed by American artist George Catlin in the course of his nineteenth century travels in North America that the native Indian mothers paid a lot of attention to their infants' breathing. If at any time the baby opened its mouth to breathe, the mother would gently press the baby's lips together to ensure continued nasal breathing. George also noted that the rate of sickness and illness among the native Indian people was very low in comparison with European settlers.

"When I have seen a poor Indian woman in the wilderness, lowering her infant from the breast, and pressing its lips together as it falls asleep… I have said to myself, 'Glorious education! Such a mother deserves to be the nurse of Emperors'. And when I have seen the careful, tender mothers in civilised life, covering the faces of their infants sleeping in overheated rooms, with their little mouths open and gasping for breath; and afterwards looked into the multitude, I have been struck with the evident evil and lasting results of this incipient," he wrote in his 'Notes of Travels Amongst the North American Indians' published in 1870.

"If A equals success,
then the formula is:
A = X + Y + Z,
X is work.
Y is play.

Z is keep your mouth shut".

Albert Einstein

A Note of Caution

Now is the time to sound a note of caution. Before breath retraining is commenced this section should be read carefully. While this is a perfectly safe therapy, it can involve an element of risk for people with particular illnesses or susceptibilities.

Please note the following in particular:

• If you experience an exacerbation of your symptoms, then you are not doing the exercises correctly and you should stop until you establish that you can do them correctly.

Do not commence breath retraining if you have any of the following conditions: sickle cell anaemia; arterial aneurysm; very high uncontrolled blood pressure; any heart problems in the past three months; uncontrolled hyperthyroidism; a known brain tumour or kidney disease.

• If you suffer from any of the following, then you should only undertake breath retraining under direct supervision of a qualified and experienced practitioner: diabetes; severe asthma; emphysema; epilepsy; schizophrenia; unsatisfactory blood pressure levels or chest pains or pain in the heart region.

If you have any of the above conditions, or if you experience any distress, or are in any way unsure, please refrain from doing exercises involving holding the breath beyond the first feeling of a need for air. Exercises involving holding the breath include nose unblocking and Steps. If you are in any doubt as to whether breath retraining may be suitable for you, please contact the Buteyko Clinic (see Appendix 5 for contact information).

What to expect;

Roughly two thirds of those who apply breath retraining will experience a cleansing reaction within the first two weeks and each time the control pause increases by ten seconds. Reduced breathing leads to an increased blood flow and better oxygenation of all internal organs especially eliminatory organs. Cleansing reactions are indicative of the powerful physiological change which the body undergoes.

People may experience symptoms such as a slight headache, diarrhoea, excessive tiredness with increased yawning, general 'flu like symptoms, insomnia, a bad taste from the mouth, foamy saliva, coloured urine, a greatly reduced appetite or a general feeling of being unwell.

This is simply your body readjusting to a healthier way of life. Symptoms are, in general, not disruptive and will pass in two or three days. Like any detoxifying process of the body, there is a short adjustment phase. Many people look forward to the reaction because it is direct feedback as their body cleanses itself after all those years of bad breathing.

Do the following to help reduce the intensity and duration of cleansing reactions:

- Drink warm water regularly throughout the day.

- Continue with reduced breathing by relaxation.

- Take pain relievers, such as a headache tablet, if necessary.

Most importantly, do not stop doing the exercises when you experience a cleansing reaction. The symptoms are a direct result of overbreathing and the control pause (explained later) will increase when the cleansing reaction has passed.

On a positive note, everyone will experience signs of health improvement including: increased calmness and concentration; better sleep and more energy, and reduced appetite and cravings for coffee, chocolate and other foodstuffs.

Nose Unblocking Exercise

A reduction in carbon dioxide levels causes an increase in mucus secretion and constriction of the airways. The following is a simple exercise which will unblock the nose in as little as five minutes. This exercise is the same for both children and adults. At this point it is worth practising the exercise before you read further.

Unblocking the nose

How to unblock
the nose;

- Sit upright on a straight-backed chair.

- Take a small breath (two seconds) in through your nose, if possible, and a small breath out (three seconds). If you are unable to take a breath in through your nose, take a tiny breath in through the corner of your mouth.

- Pinch your nose and hold your breath. Keep your mouth closed.

- Gently nod your head or sway your body until you feel that you cannot hold your breath any longer. (Hold your nose until you feel a relatively strong need for air.)

- When you need to breathe in, let go of your nose and breathe gently through it, in and out, with your mouth closed. Avoid taking a deep breath when you breathe in, and calm your breathing as soon as possible by focusing on relaxation. Repeat to yourself "relax and breathe less".

- Continue to do this exercise until you can breathe through your nose fully. If your nose does not become totally unblocked, wait about two minutes and perform this exercise again. Initially you may need to do this a number of times before your nose is completely unblocked. This is yet another case of 'practice makes perfect'.

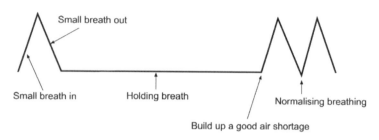

How to unblock the nose naturally

After doing this exercise a few times your nose will be unblocked. If you continue to overbreathe, or take a deep breath, you will lose the additional carbon dioxide and your nose will become blocked again. Perform this exercise each time that your nose becomes blocked. Even if you have a cold, make sure to breathe through your nose. You may think you can't clear your nose when you have a heavy cold, but you can.

When the switch is first made from mouth to nasal breathing, the volume of air being inhaled will reduce. The body may begin to play tricks and convince individuals to breathe more by inducing yawning, sighing, regular sniffing or the odd mouth breath. Try not to increase breathing at this point.

When the need to deep breathe arises, for example during a sigh, swallow immediately. If the need to yawn also occurs, avoid taking the deep breath that accompanies a yawn. Instead stifle the yawn by keeping the mouth closed, or swallow.

It takes just a few days for a habitual mouth breather to change breathing to permanent nose breathing. Increasing observation of breathing, reducing volume of breathing and practising nose unblocking exercises are important elements in trying to make this change.

After the change to nasal breathing has been made, it will become uncomfortable to mouth breathe because the effects of cold dry air entering through the mouth will be felt. Often people begin to wonder how on earth they managed to go through life with a permanent, and very uncomfortable, blocked nose - a condition which is frequently, and usually unsuccessfully, addressed by the use of nasal sprays, decongestants or even an operation.

Nasal remedy

Those suffering constant nasal congestion and inflammation should practice nose unblocking exercises but also wash out the nose daily with the following remedy - especially those who have become dependent on nasal sprays.

Dissolve half a teaspoon of sea salt and half a teaspoon of bread soda (bicarbonate) in one pint of boiled water and let it cool. A plastic syringe with a rubber bulb can be purchased from a pharmacy. Fill this syringe with the solution and squeeze into one nostril while blocking the other nostril with a finger. Sniff the water in until it reaches the back of the throat. Spit it out and then repeat with the other nostril.

Another option is to cup the warm salt water into the hand and sniff the water up into the nose one nostril at a time (again with the other nostril blocked).

People who live near the sea find that sniffing up clean sea water is also effective. This is a traditional remedy which also works well for sinus problems.

Yogi have, for thousands of years, realised the benefits of nasal cleansing and use a special vessel called a neti pot to pour the solution into each nostril.

How big do you breathe?

Buteyko Clinic is a program of breath retraining aimed at reversing chronic hyperventilation on a permanent basis. While the exercises are very simple, it is important to follow them exactly as they are written in order to experience maximum benefits.

With breath retraining, there are two measurements that are used to monitor your progress. These are the **pulse** and the **control pause [CP]**.

Pulse

The pulse is measured by counting the number of heartbeats per minute. Another option is to measure the number of beats over thirty seconds and multiply by two. When measuring heartbeats, make sure to measure your pulse and not to count the number of seconds on your clock or watch.

Locate the pulse about one inch up from the wrist and about one centimetre inwards on the thumb side of the hand. Place two fingers from the free hand onto the groove or channel in this area of the wrist where the slight throb of the pulse can be felt through the fingertips.

If you have difficulty locating the pulse on the wrist then check for it at the carotid artery in the neck.

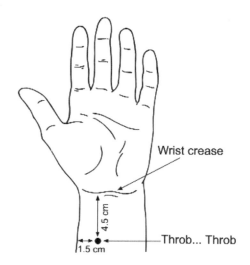

Wrist crease

4.5 cm

Throb... Throb

1.5 cm

Measuring the pulse

In general, the lower the resting heart rate, the healthier the individual is. Normal healthy adults will have a pulse rate of 60 to 80 beats per minute at rest.

Physically fit individuals will have a lower pulse rate than this, although some individuals have a naturally low pulse rate.

The normal pulse range for a child is higher than that of an adult. A child's pulse can vary from 60 to 100 beats per minute which decreases as the child gets older.

It is advisable to note that the aforementioned pulse rate measurements must be only taken after resting for half-an-hour as the pulse rate increases considerably with physical activity.

The pulse will vary depending on a variety of factors. It may be adversely affected by, for example, food consumption levels, food allergies, stimulants such as coffee or chocolate, and factors such as excitement, anxiety, excessive talking and, of course, big breathing.

**The bigger the breathing volume
- the higher the pulse**

**A correct breathing volume
- A low pulse**

**In general a low pulse
means good fitness levels**

Control pause [CP]

The control pause is a measure of the level of carbon dioxide in the alveoli based on a comfortable breath hold.

By reducing the volume of breathing, carbon dioxide levels increase and therefore the control pause will increase. Through overbreathing, the carbon dioxide level will decrease and therefore the control pause will decrease. The control pause will also decrease if medication is reduced too drastically.

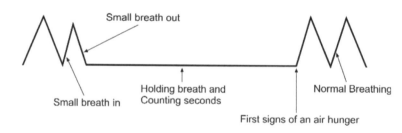

Small breath out

Small breath in

Holding breath and
Counting seconds

First signs of an air hunger

Normal Breathing

Measuring your control pause- for this you will need a watch or a clock with a second hand

• Sit in an upright chair and adopt a good posture. Relax your shoulders and rest your lower back against the back of the chair.

- Take a small breath in (two seconds) and a small breath out (three seconds).

- Hold your nose on the 'out' breath, with empty lungs but not too empty. Holding your nose is necessary to prevent air entering into the airways.

- Count how many seconds you can comfortably last before you need to breathe in again. Release your nose and breathe in through it.

- Your first intake of breath after the CP should be no greater than your breath prior to taking measurement; you should not hold your breath for too long as this may cause you to take a big breath after measuring the CP.

Measuring the Control Pause (b)

43

Carbon dioxide level

The level of carbon dioxide in the body determines the length of time the breath can be held: a higher level of carbon dioxide corresponds to a longer breath hold. The table below was developed by Professor Buteyko after he had measured the breath-holding ability of literally thousands of patients and matched it to their carbon dioxide levels. The figures are consistent and show the level of carbon dioxide based on the length of the control pause.

	CO_2 in alveoli [%]	Control pause [sec]
Perfect Health	6.5	60
	6.0	50
Good health	5.5	40
	5.0	30
	4.5	20
Poor health	4.0	10
	3.5	5
	Death	

A sick person will have a low CP
The lower the CP, the poorer the health

**A healthy person will have
a high CP**

From week to week, there should be a noticeable improvement in the control pause. The body will become conditioned to a higher level of carbon dioxide when breathing exercises are practised correctly. This will be reflected in a higher control pause. As far as Buteyko breathing is concerned, the control pause is the most important measurement of an individual's health.

Increase in your CP- health is improving

Decrease in your CP- health is deteriorating

Measuring the CP in the morning before breakfast gives the most important measurement of the state of a person's health. In the depths of sleep, breathing is a subconscious activity that cannot be interfered with. For this reason, the morning CP will give a true measurement of the level of carbon dioxide.

How many people do you breathe for?

- If your morning control pause is less than ten seconds then you have a breathing volume greater than six times your body's requirements.

- If your morning control pause is 15 to 20 seconds you are breathing four times the body's requirements.

- If your morning control pause is 20 to 30 seconds you are breathing three times the body's requirements.

- If your morning control pause is 30 to 40 seconds you are breathing one-and-a-half times to twice the body's requirements.

- If your morning control pause is 40 to 60 seconds, then your breathing is correct.

If your morning control pause is sixty seconds you have no health problems or diseases of civilisation. For over forty years Professor Buteyko and his associates were unable to find any person with a control pause of sixty seconds who had any of the diseases of modern civilisation. Diseases of civilisation are those which have become more widespread as countries become more industrialised, including angina, asthma, allergies, bronchitis, bronchiectasis, chronic fatigue syndrome, diabetes, emphysema, hypertension, sleep apnoea and many more.

Compare our lifestyles

Fifty years ago;

Greater physical activity

More natural foods

Cooler temperatures of houses

Less stress- green environment

Result – Correct volume breathing- Higher CP-

Diseases of civilisation uncommon

Today

Little physical activity

More processed foods

Higher temperatures of houses

More stress- concrete environment

Result - Big volume breathing - Lower CP -

Diseases of civilisation very common

"The end of the human race will be that it will eventually die of civilization".-Ralph Waldo Emerson

Chapter 3

Taking Control

"'Begin at the beginning,' the king said gravely, 'and go till you come to the end; then stop.'"

- Lewis Carroll, Alice's Adventures in Wonderland

To trap a higher level of carbon dioxide and to readjust the respiratory centre to this increased amount, exercises specifically aimed at reducing breathing are performed at specific times each day. When you are able to maintain a control pause of forty seconds, you will have mastered the art of correct breathing, it will be an unconscious activity, and will be incorporated into your daily life.

To increase the control pause to your interim target of twenty seconds, **breathing exercises are essential**. As you train yourself to breathe correctly, **physical activity should be used** in conjunction with breathing exercises to help increase the control pause from twenty to your ultimate aim of forty seconds.

The objective:

O ver a twelve-month period, breathing is brought to the more normal level of three to five litres as shown in the following diagram. This breathing is best described as regular, calm and smooth.

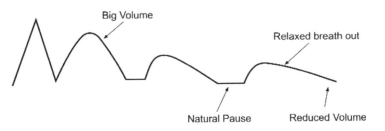

The change to correct breathing

I have included in this book a number of different breathing exercises. Choosing the most appropriate depends on a number of factors, such as whether you are an adult or a child, and whether or not you are physically exercising at the time.

As you read on, you will see that three breathing exercises are outlined in this chapter as follows:

Reduced breathing for adults.
Reduced breathing for children.
Reduced breathing when blowing your nose.

Reduced breathing for adults

The following is a very simplified version of one of the main exercises involved in breath correction. Certain steps have been omitted as it is essential they are practiced under the direct supervision of a practitioner to take into account individual nuances of the patient.

Exercises should be carried out in a quiet place with no distractions. The temperature should be cool and the room airy because a hot and stuffy environment can promote big breathing, the exact opposite of what you are trying to achieve.

Finger under the nose

F ood affects your breathing, so it is not recommended that you practice immediately after eating a meal. Exercises are best practised before meals or at least two hours after them.

• Adopt a correct but comfortable posture. Correct posture involves sitting up straight with both feet underneath your chair. If you have difficulty with this, then imagine a thread suspended from the ceiling, attached to the top of your head, holding you in an upright position. Correct posture is very important in helping to reduce your breathing.

• Now feel the movement of air in and out of your body, particularly through your nostrils. Concentrate on the slight movement your body makes with each inhalation and exhalation. It is vital to be aware of your breathing so that you can correct it. If you are unaware of your breathing, you will not be able to improve it.

• As you breathe, let your shoulders fall to their natural position. Raised or tense shoulders increase the volume of the chest cavity and so increase the volume of air inhaled. Tension increases breathing, but relaxation decreases it.

• The next step is to monitor the amount of air flowing through your nostrils by placing your finger under your nose in a horizontal position. Your finger should lie just above your top lip, and close enough to your nostrils so that you can feel the airflow, but not so close that the air-flow is blocked.

• Now, breathe air slightly into the tip of your nostrils. Little breaths or short breaths mean the amount of air reaching your lungs reduces. By reducing the length of each breath, the number of breaths you take every minute may increase, but don' t worry because this is normal. Remember that the aim is to reduce the volume.

• When you breathe out, the more warm air you feel, the bigger your breathing. Concentrate on reducing the amount of warm air you feel on your finger.

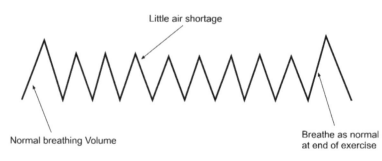

Creating a Little air shortage

Don't worry if this exercise does not work for you the first time you try it. Over time it will become easier. A gradual and relaxed approach is best, because if you try to decrease the amount of air too quickly or too much, it may cause involuntary gasps of air or cause you to take bigger breaths. It is important that you get to the stage where you can sustain reduced breathing over the course of three to five minutes.

Take a few minutes' break before you start the next five minutes of reduced breathing. One set of twenty minutes per day is the **minimum** time that should be spent on this exercise, combined with relaxation and observation of your breathing for the remainder of the day and night (more about this later). In order to make progress it is necessary to spend this amount of time practising. After a number of weeks, and depending on your progress, breathing exercises can be performed while doing any activity such as reading a book or watching television.

A block of exercises consists of:

1. Take your pulse, and note it.

2. Control pause.

3. Reduced breathing for five minutes.

4. Control pause.

5. Reduced breathing for five minutes.

6. Control pause.

7. Reduced breathing for five minutes.

8. Control pause.

9. Reduced breathing for five minutes.

10. Control pause.

11. Check your pulse again and compare with your pulse rate when you started the exercise.

Your **control pause should increase** and **pulse decrease** when the exercises have been completed.

Summary of reduced breathing for adults

- Set aside time when you will have no distractions.

- Sit down and adopt the correct posture.

- Place your finger under your nose without blocking the air-flow.

- Concentrate on reducing the amount of air that is blown onto your finger by monitoring the temperature of the air you are breathing out through your nose.

- Reduce volume by taking very small breaths.

- Your **control pause should increase** when the exercises have been completed.

- Your **pulse should decrease** when the exercises have been completed.

Reduced breathing for children

We use a different method, called 'Steps', to help children understand the process of improving their carbon dioxide levels, simply because children may have difficulty using reduced breathing for adults.

For the purposes explaining this exercise, let's imagine again that you're dealing with a child called Emily.

Doing steps

To perform *Steps* Emily should:

● Take a small breath in for two seconds and a small breath out lasting three seconds.

● Hold her breath by pinching her nose. It's better if Emily holds her nose by raising her hand above her mouth so that her mouth is visible. This way, if she takes a breath in through her mouth, it will be noticed.

● Get her to walk as many steps as she can until she needs to breathe in again. During *Steps*, encourage Emily to build up a large air shortage by doing as many steps as she can manage before she breathes in.

● To encourage Emily to walk as many as possible count aloud every five or ten steps. Ensure she doesn't overdo it. If she does, it could become too stressful for her, and could put her off the exercises altogether.

● When Emily starts breathing, it must be only through her nose and her breathing must be calmed immediately. If her shoulders rise or become tense, point this out to her, and ask her to let her shoulders drop to the normal resting position.

● After completing *Steps* the first breath will usually be bigger than normal. Make sure Emily reduces or suppresses the second and third breaths.

• Get her to relax, by explaining that a relaxed body is like jelly on a plate, so that there is no tension and the muscles go all floppy. The more Emily relaxes, the quicker will be her recovery of normal breathing.

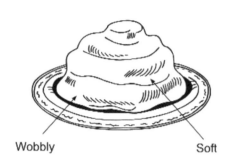

Wobbly

Soft

Learning to relax

• Count each step aloud and record the number. Compare each day's steps with the previous day's so that progress can be measured.

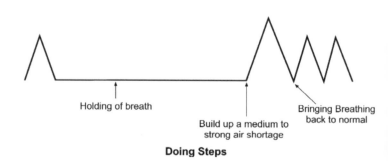

Holding of breath

Build up a medium to strong air shortage

Bringing Breathing back to normal

Doing Steps

Measurement tool

If a child is unable to do the control pause correctly, the *Steps* exercise - the best way of increasing carbon dioxide levels - can be used as a measurement tool. Always encourage the child to increase their steps over time. The goal is for the child to be able to walk a hundred paces without having to take a breath. *Steps* should be done only while walking. Reasonably fast walking is fine, but the child should not run.

Two to three lines of *Steps* should be practised each day in order to reach this goal. If the child has severe asthma or is feeling unwell however, then steps must be only practised under direct supervision of a Buteyko Clinic practitioner.

Again, the best times for the *Steps* exercises are before breakfast in the morning and at night, just before going to bed.

Everyone knows children can have a short attention span so if the child becomes bored with doing exercises, then Steps can be replaced with breath-holding while playing hopscotch, squats, jumping jacks or swimming (in the case of swimming, aim to increase the amount of strokes or time spent under water between each breath).

The Jumps

Correct sequence for children

CP	Steps	Steps	Steps	CP	Steps	Steps	Steps	CP

Rest for about one minute between each set of *Steps*.

Summary of steps

● Take a small breath in (two seconds) and a small breath out (three seconds).
● Hold the breath and walk as many steps as possible until there is a strong desire to breathe in again.
● After completion of steps relax like jelly.
● Count aloud each step and record the number so that progress can be monitored.
● Steps can be used as a measurement of progress.

Reduced breathing when blowing your nose

Every time you blow your nose, some carbon dioxide is lost. Blowing your nose too much will result in an excessive loss of carbon dioxide. This will lead to an increase in the production of mucus, and you will then blow your nose to clear the mucus, resulting in a further loss of carbon dioxide, which will in turn create more mucus. Like coughing, blowing the nose can be the catalyst for a vicious circle of nose clearing, carbon dioxide loss and mucus creation.

• Try not to blow your nose but, if you must, do so only when absolutely necessary.

• Blow your nose gently. Blowing your nose forcibly causes a greater loss of carbon dioxide and can also exacerbate sinus or ear problems.

• After blowing your nose, hold your breath for a period equal to roughly half the length of your control pause.

• Reduce your breathing.

• For a child, do a set of *Steps* as outlined in Exercise Two in this chapter.

Chapter 4

Make Correct Breathing a Habit

"The beginning of a habit is like an invisible thread, but every time we repeat the act we strengthen the strand, add to it another filament, until it becomes a great cable and binds us irrevocably, thought and act."

- Orison Swett Marden

Physical exercise, talking, laughing and even sleeping influence our breathing patterns. In fact, everyday activities all have a role to play in the way we breathe so therefore it is necessary that we reduce the possibility of hyperventilation during them.

This chapter is sub-divided into:

Correct breathing while speaking.

Reduced breathing while sleeping.

The breathing muscles.

A strategy for abdominal breathing.

Correct breathing while speaking

People who regularly cough will be aware that their coughing can be triggered by speaking for a period of time. Frequently at workshops people remark: "my coughing really starts at a meeting, or when I speak for long periods." Other people will be aware of how tired they feel following a day spent talking.

Here are some suggestions which will help in addressing this problem:

• Be aware of the need to **minimise** the amount of talking you do.

• Try not to take a **big breath** in through your mouth prior to talking.

• Long sentences result in a large exhalation of carbon dioxide, so aim to shorten your sentences.

• Aim to ensure that your breathing is quiet while you are talking because noisy breathing is indicative of overbreathing.

• Observe how other people breathe while they speak. This will help you with your own breathing techniques. Look out for sharp inhalations of air and movement of the upper chest while others talk.

Laughter is the best medicine

Laughter has been described as the best medicine for many ills, but you must learn to control your breathing during it. Constant laughter involves deep inhalations and exhalations causing a loss of carbon dioxide. A number of experts have recognised the role of laughter in contributing to asthma symptoms.

During laughter, try to:

• Reduce fits of laughter.

• Laugh with your mouth closed.

• Breathe in only through your nose.

• Hold your breath afterwards for a few seconds to replenish any loss of carbon dioxide.

Sometimes you just have to give way to a fit of laughter; you can't help it. But do help yourself to get your breath back by reducing your breathing.

Correct breathing during sleeping

Many patients tell me that their symptoms are worse during the night or first thing in the morning. Some even say that it takes them hours every morning to get their breathing right. Symptoms such as a blocked nose, excessive mucus, tiredness, chest tightness, wheezing and breathlessness are common. These problems are usually caused by incorrect breathing while sleeping, and it is for this reason that we need to pay particular attention to how we breathe when we are asleep.

Big breathing at night contributes to:

Snoring

Sleep apnoea

Disrupted sleep

Bed wetting

Having to get up to go to the loo during the night

Unable to get out of bed in the morning

Tiredness during the day

The risk of a coughing, wheezing or heart attack is greatest during sleep. Statistics show that most attacks occur between the hours of 3.00 and 5.00 a.m.. Professor Buteyko's theory is that the **natural position for humans is upright** because when we lie down, our breathing increases automatically in comparison with the needs of our metabolism. For someone who is already overbreathing, this further increase in breathing will lead to a further depletion of carbon dioxide levels.

Oversleeping is not good either. A good rule of thumb is to sleep only when you feel tired. This is when your body is telling you that sleep is necessary and generally seven to eight hours per night is enough. If you feel the need to sleep during the day, take a nap for twenty minutes while sitting upright.

Correct breathing will increase your energy level and reduce fatigue so additional sleep should not be necessary. As your CP increases, the number of hours sleep you need each night should gradually decrease - probably to somewhere between five or six.

Reduced breathing during the day will help to reduce overbreathing at night, but we have very little control of our breathing in the depths of our slumbers. Because of this, there are a number of recommendations that may be followed to help ensure correct breathing at night.

Sleeping positions

Sleeping on your back is generally the worst position. Your lower jaw drops and mouth breathing is almost inevitable. In this position, there is very little restriction to breathing and so breathing becomes bigger. Snoring, which is also caused by overbreathing and breathing through the mouth, is worse while sleeping on your back.

Increased blood pressure and bad health are just some of the side effects of snoring, not to mention the strain it can put on even the most harmonious of marriages. (I was in a youth hostel one night many years ago where a severe snorer was in danger of suffering grievous bodily harm from the adjoining bunk - and the general consensus was that he would have deserved it!)

Another condition which affects children especially is bed wetting. For years Buteyko advocated that bed wetting was caused by hyperventilation. Now new research, published in *New Scientist*, confirms his view: "Breathing problems are to blame for many cases of bedwetting in children, and perhaps in some adults too. And a simple treatment might solve the problem within weeks."[1]

Sleeping on the back with mouth open

Changing from sleeping on your back to sleeping on your side may take some time. It may be helpful to place a number of pillows behind you while you sleep on your side. Another suggestion would be to wear a rucksack on your back filled with clothes or a football, and then there is the old wives' tale of sewing a tennis or golf ball into the back of your nightwear. All of these options may sound a little eccentric, but they will reduce the likelihood of you rolling onto your back and you should, over time, switch to sleeping on your side or tummy.

After years of research, Professor Buteyko came to the conclusion that people who sleep on their left side, in the foetal position, tend to breathe less deeply. A hard mattress, which restricts frontal movement of the body, can also help to reduce breathing. A soft mattress, particularly something like a water bed, is not good for correct breathing because it offers too little resistance.

**Sleeping on left side with
closed mouth**

Never eat before sleep

Eating a meal or drinking a protein-rich drink such as milk or hot chocolate two or even three hours before going to bed will result in increased breathing. Then you will have both an increase in breathing due to lying in a horizontal position, and an increase in breathing due to eating or drinking. Then over-breathing is guaranteed, resulting in a poor night's sleep.

Eating late at night on a regular basis is inherently unhealthy for anyone - asthmatic or not. It can cause a heart attack or a stroke, contributes to increased weight gain and lethargy, and it can disrupt the appetite the following day. My grandfather was a man of much wisdom and he had a saying that you should "always wake up with an appetite". I'm sure he was right.

Breathing through the nose at night

While sleeping it is important to breathe only through your nose. Mouth breathing will reverse the benefits of reduced breathing during the day. **If you neglect your breathing for seven or eight hours every night then it will be impossible to change your breathing pattern on a permanent basis.**

Here are some suggestions which will help you make a permanent switch to nasal breathing while sleeping:

- **The guardian angel**

One suggestion which may be suitable for children, is to have someone watch over you until you become more used to breathing through your nose at night. The role of this person is to close your mouth gently when you begin to mouth breathe, or to wake you if your breathing becomes too deep. A confirmed insomniac might fill the bill; otherwise, good luck in your search for a guardian angel!

• The hat or scarf

For children get a hat with a strap that comes under the chin. Cut most of the material from the hat so that there is just enough to keep the structure intact. Cutting away as much material as possible prevents the child from becoming too warm during the night because this would contribute to overbreathing. Get the child to wear the hat to bed and bring the strap under the chin to stop the lower jaw dropping down. A variation on this theme is to wrap a scarf around the child's head and under the chin. Tie it to ensure that the lower jaw is unable to drop down during the night. Both of these suggestions could be consigned to the 'off the wall' category by image-conscious children. However, with these suggestions in mind Buteyko Clinic is currently in the process of having a special type of headwear designed to allow nighttime nasal breathing with minimum discomfort.

• Paper tape

From my experience, this is the idea that works best. Taping was first suggested by Buteyko's patients and has been used successfully by thousands of people in Russia, Australia, New Zealand and the UK. If you feel that the tape is not for you, then use any of the above options (or one of your own) to prevent mouth breathing during the night.

The idea is to tape over the mouth with some sort of sticky paper. Make sure your mouth is completely closed before applying the tape. If your mouth is partially open, then you will be able to breathe through the tape during the night. I have found that the most suitable tape is 1 inch Micropore which can be purchased at most chemists. Apply it horizontally to cover the mouth. If you are unable to place it in a horizontal position, then place it vertically. Before placing, remove much of the glue on it by sticking the tape to your hand and peeling it off a number of times. Do this until there is just enough glue to hold the tape in place. Before placing the tape on your mouth, make two tabs by putting a small fold at two of the corners. This will ease the task of removing the tape in the morning. The tape should not to be used on a child less than five years of age, and any child using it must be able to remove the tape during the night if they feel they need to.

The tape should not be used if you are feeling nauseous or if you have been drinking alcohol.

If you are having difficulty breathing during the night while using the tape, then do reduced breathing exercises. Try not to remove the tape as, if you do, you are likely to begin to mouth breathe during your sleep and this will only make your symptoms worse.

It is possible that some people may, very reasonably, experience a feeling of panic at the very thought of having their mouth taped. To help overcome this it may be helpful to put the tape on half an hour before going to bed. This should be enough time to become used to the tape and to overcome any nervousness. For the first few nights wearing the tape will feel a little strange. It may come off during the night, but at least you will have spent some hours breathing through your nose. Continue to wear the tape until you have managed to change to breathing through your nose at night. How long this takes will vary with the individual.

If your nose is partially blocked before going to bed, then first clear your nose by completing the nose unblocking exercise outlined earlier. While wearing the tape, your nose will never completely block. If you are breathing deeply during the night while wearing the tape, your nose will partially block. This is the body's defence mechanism to prevent over breathing. However, when the nose becomes partially blocked, the level of carbon dioxide in the body will increase and this will unblock the nose. If you continue to overbreathe, your nose will become partially blocked again which will increase the level of carbon dioxide thus causing the nose to unblock and so on. Remember, your nose will only block completely if you switch to mouth breathing.

REMINDER

Do not use the tape on a child if the child is unable to remove it easily themselves, or is unhappy about it. Do not use the tape if you are feeling nauseous, or have been doing any serious drinking.

Indicators of mouth breathing whilst sleeping

You will know you are mouth breathing if:

- You wake up during the night breathing through your mouth, or
- Your mouth is dry in the morning.

Summary of correct sleeping

- Try to sleep on your left side.

- Never eat late at night. Don't be afraid to go to bed hungry; it won't do you any harm.

- Breathe only through the nose at night.

- Avoid central heating in the bedroom.

Our breathing muscles

The three main groups of muscles used for breathing are the diaphragm, intercostal and accessory. Adopting diaphragmatic breathing is important for reducing hyperventilation.

The diaphragm is a strong, thin, flat sheet of muscle which separates the chest from the tummy and is shaped like the dome of an umbrella. The downward movement of the diaphragm on the abdominal contents causes the stomach to expand a little as we breathe in.

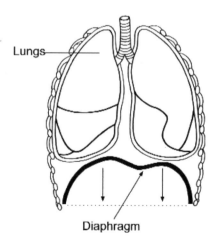

The Diaphragm

Two activities which result in poor use of the diaphragm are bad posture and mouth breathing. Mouth breathers tend to breathe using their upper chest muscles. Switching to nasal breathing is the first step in changing to diaphragmatic breathing.

Poor posture has a negative impact on breathing and being slouched over a desk all day will not help.

'Deep' versus 'big'

The correct interpretation of the word 'deep' in this context is breathing using the diaphragm. A deep breath means using the depth of the lungs. There is a misconception that a deep breath is a big breath. A deep breath can be a big or a small breath. What is important is that the diaphragm moves. From time to time, I ask people to take a deep breath and the response is almost always huge inhalations of air - often through the mouth. Not only is this breathing big, it is also shallow as chest muscles predominate and only the top parts of the lungs are ventilated.

"As we free our breath (through diaphragmatic breathing) we relax our emotions and let go our body tensions."

- Gay Hendricks

Strategy for abdominal breathing:

For this exercise, do not wear a very tight fitting belt, or clothes that will restrict abdominal breathing. It may help if you open the top button of your trousers if it is unduly restrictive.

- Sit up straight and adopt a correct posture.

- Have both feet flat on the floor.

- Relax your shoulders and upper chest; this is very important.

- Imagine that the back of your head is lightly suspended by a thread from the ceiling.

- Lengthen the distance from your sternum (chest bone) to your navel.

- With your lips lightly together, breathe in gently through your nose.

- Place one hand on your chest and one hand on your tummy.

- Concentrate on having very little movement of the upper chest.

- Gradually reduce the amount of movement in

your chest; having your hand on your chest will register this.

- With your other hand, direct your attention to feeling your tummy move out with each inhalation and in on each exhalation.

- Repeat to yourself: breathe out - tummy in; breathe in - tummy out.

OUT - IN
IN - OUT

- Imagine a loose elastic band around your waist stretching slightly (but only slightly) as you inhale, and contracting as you exhale.

- Focus on your stomach expanding with each inhalation and contracting with each exhalation. These movements are noticeable but slight.

Practice this for ten minutes each day, in addition to your exercises, until you have reduced upper chest breathing considerably. It is important not to practice for more than ten minutes at a time because breathing muscles can become very tired.

Chapter 5

Breathe Right During Physical Activity

"A man's health can be judged by which he takes two at a time-- pills or stairs."

- Joan Welsh

The importance
of exercise

It is important to note that depending on the severity of your condition, and on your general medical history, you may need to check with your doctor before starting a new exercise regime.

The human body was designed to lead a physically active life, therefore continued good health and well-being requires some degree of exercise. Over the years research has consistently shown that, compared to those who take little or no exercise, people who exercise regularly are healthier, live longer, have greater inner calmness, are more content and cope better with life's stresses and strains.

There are two big differences between our lifestyle and that of a couple of generations ago: they tended to eat less and more healthily and had a far more physically active lifestyle (even if they had never heard the phrase).

Nowadays we have fallen into a sedentary routine - one that is having a disastrous effect on the health of the nation. Few of us walk or cycle to work, we drive or are driven and few of us have jobs that require much serious physical effort. Many of us do take exercise during our free time but many more are addicted to TV and/or the pub culture.

Our Lifestyle- not so long ago

Most of our day is spent sitting and, as if this wasn't enough for the body to contend with, we then add stress, smoking, overeating and eating inappropriately. It is no wonder that the population of the western world is becoming less and less healthy and, as a result, putting more and more pressure on national health services.

Six hours per day watching TV – is this what life is about?

As one commentator suggested: "If it weren't for the fact that the TV set and the refrigerator are so far apart, some of us wouldn't get any exercise at all."

What sort of exercise?

It seems that the answer to the question is: whatever sort of exercise you like. Commencing exercise after a long period of minimal physical activity requires a number of points to be considered first.

Go for something you like doing, or could get to like. **Slow and steady is the way to go.** Don't be too ambitious when starting off, but do try to progress week to week - walk, or cycle, jog or swim further, a little faster and for longer.

Exercise within your capabilities. Try not to miss a day - make your daily exercise routine a priority. Beware of over training, you won't enjoy it and it won't help you in the longer term. Get out into the open air whenever you can, it's healthier and also enjoying yourself will help you to feel better.

We should exercise because we enjoy it and because we feel better for it. Adopting the attitude that "taking exercise is a drag" will make success difficult. Even if the physical activity is not enjoyable at first because it may represent a major lifestyle change, try to stick with it or perhaps try a different activity. Eventually it will become enjoyable; after all, it is what the body was designed for.

Life's greatest pleasures are often the simple ones. Walking in the peace of the countryside, listening to the music that nature provides, is one. Introducing children to the everyday wonders of nature is the greatest gift they can be given. Help them to appreciate bird song or to watch out for native animals - rabbits, foxes, hares - going about their daily business. There are still busy ducks and majestic swans on the country's lakes and rivers and it is possible to still catch the occasional glimpse or hear the splash of a fish jumping. There is great and simple pleasure in the natural world for any age.

Humans are built for motion

Depending on which part of the country you live in, it is possible to walk by the sea, along a river or canal bank, or by the shores of a lake and there are still country lanes not infested with speeding traffic.

Alternatively just walk around your own town or city - you should be able to find somewhere to go and you may even have a park nearby.

If personal preference or necessity, or a sociable nature, means opting for the indoors alternative then a gym is the next best thing. The exercise bike is a good alternative to cycling on roads (and a lot safer), rowing machines are pleasant to use, climbing machines are easier on the joints than the treadmills but there's a whole range of exercise options available.

How do you know if you are exercising correctly?

You are exercising correctly if you can achieve the following: nasal breathing, an improved control pause and if you no longer require reliever medication prior to exercise.

Nasal breathing: It is of the utmost importance that all breathing is done only through the nose. This comes as quite a shock to most people because mouth breathing is so predominant in every activity, including walking.

When the change to nasal breathing is first made fitness levels will tend to dip below the normal level. However with continued nasal breathing this will soon correct itself. Research conducted with top athletes has shown that fitness levels will improve substantially within eight weeks if nasal breathing is maintained. It is advisable for people involved in sports to train at a more relaxed pace until they become accustomed to nasal breathing. Once the new regime becomes like second nature more intensive training can be undertaken.

When the CP is low, as soon as the need to breathe in through the mouth arises, it is important to stop and relax, wait for a few minutes to catch a breath and only then proceed with the exercise once again. It is only when the CP is high, that mouth breathing can prevail for a short duration of time.

It is often pointed out that nasal breathing can become quite pronounced and audible during even mild exercise. The body's requirement for air increases substantially with any exercise. As a result the breathing becomes louder and many people are conscious that other people can hear them breathing while they are out walking. This is only a temporary state and breathing will reduce as the levels of carbon dioxide increase. Whatever happens it is important not to revert to mouth breathing.

Remember;

Low CP- **nasal breathe only**
High CP- **can mouth breathe**
for short period

Controlled breathing during sports

It is relatively easy to combine controlled breathing with sport, with the exception of sports that require intensive bursts such as sprinting. For example, playing football should not present a problem if a gentle and gradual warm-up is performed first.

Other steps to aid breathing can also be taken during the match. When the ball is elsewhere, breathe a little less than is required and when running for the ball try to keep breathing through the nose. If it gets to the stage where the need arises to breathe through the mouth, calm the breathing and switch to nasal breathing as soon as the ball has been passed. If the need to breathe through the mouth for long periods occurs, then it is better to stop playing football until such breathing becomes easier and it is possible to play at the desired level. Continuing to play while not breathing properly will not help. So while playing try to ensure the breathing is not too deep and remember to observe the breathing pattern as much as possible.

Walking for half an hour every day is probably the best exercise for anyone who has not been taking regular exercise. Initially it may be best to walk alone rather than having to keep pace with someone else. Walking alone also avoids talking which promotes mouth breathing and increases hyperventilation. While walking, breathing should be reduced and again if at any time the need to deep breathe is experienced while walking or doing any exercise, then slow down and relax. Resist the urge to breathe through the mouth and, instead, stop and calm the breathing and when ready start walking again.

Those people whose health is poor and who can only walk around twenty paces should start by just walking fifteen paces and stopping. Breathing should be reduced and it is important never to push the body beyond the point where breathing cannot be controlled; to do so would be counter-productive and potentially dangerous. Don't be too concerned by needing to start at a very modest level; perseverance will result in being able to gradually walk further and further.

Coaches and trainers take note

It is a common misconception that big breathing is good for our health and this arises nowhere more than in the area of sport and training. Many coaches mistakenly believe that taking big breaths in through the nose and out through the mouth is beneficial and the theory is that toxins in the lungs will be removed by exhalation. Sports people can be seen in gyms around the country taking intentional big breaths as they lift weights and force a breath out through the mouth as the weight is relaxed. Instructors regularly advise during a warm down to breathe in through the nose and out through the mouth. Why is this bad habit so deeply ingrained despite the fact no one has ever benefited from it?

Big breathing in this manner not only reduces oxygenation of tissues due to the role of carbon dioxide as a catalyst for the release of oxygen, but may also contribute to dehydration. The nose contains turbinates and a mucus blanket that serves to remove moisture as air is exhaled from the body. To illustrate this, breathe out through your mouth onto a glass surface and check to see how much moisture content is left on the glass. Do this a second time, but this time breathe out through your nose. The amount of moisture left after the mouth breath is far greater than that left after the nose breath. A loss of moisture from the body contributes to dehydration, and dehydrated airways can be very sensitive to various stimuli.

Sports instructors who take the initiative and apply this therapy will notice a dramatic improvement in the fitness levels of all students. Reduced breathing has been taught to a number of people involved in various sports at the top level. In every situation, recovery times have improved, lactic acid build up has reduced, the pulse rate has been reduced and overall fitness levels have been improved. In an area of such competitive pressure where fractions of seconds can make the difference between winning and losing, athletes who apply this therapy will have an advantage over their peers.

It is not what you do, but how you do it

No matter what sport or exercise is chosen, adhere to the following: be able to maintain control of your breathing at all times; be able to perform exercise with nasal breathing; feel good throughout the exercise, and enjoy it.

For example, the exercises quite often found to be most suitable are walking, jogging, cycling and lifting modest weights. Sports such as sprinting involve huge bursts of energy and require panting and mouth breathing.

The higher the CP, the greater the fitness level

The lower the CP, the poorer the fitness level

Summary of behaviour during sports and physical exercise

- Exercise regularly and within your capabilities.

- Walking or lifting light dumbbells / weights is excellent.

- Nasal breathe during exercises.

- Do not spend fourteen hours of your day sitting down like a lot of unhealthy people do.

Chapter 6

Food that Helps,
Food that Hurts

"Let your food be
your medicine."

- Hippocrates, 400 B.C..

Food plays a large part in our lives and so diet deserves special attention because it is certainly a contributory factor in causing overbreathing.

All food increases our breathing, some foods more than others, but water does not affect respiration.

By carrying out breathing exercises properly you may experience a **substantial reduction in appetite.** This is because your body is better able to absorb nutrients from food due to increased oxygenation and improved blood supply to the gastrointestinal tract. Food then serves as a provider of essential nutrients as opposed to feeding disease. An old saying is: "Of the food we eat, one third is for bodily requirements and two thirds is for the doctor". Along with increased observation of breathing, pay attention to your body's requirement for food. When you do feel a reduction in appetite, do not force yourself to eat as this will slow down your progress.

With breathing exercises and normalisation of CO2, people who are overweight will reduce weight naturally, effortlessly and quickly.

Diet guidelines

Do not overeat

Only eat when you feel hungry. Eating when you are not hungry means that your body uses energy in order to process food that it does not need. This leads to increased breathing and is not good for your health.

Stop eating when you feel you have had enough. Overeating will increase the risk factors for chronic degenerative disease such as cancer, diabetes, heart disease, and arthritic diseases. It has been well documented that reducing food intake will promote longevity of life. Reducing calorie intake while meeting your body's requirements of nutrients is the secret to a better and longer life. Remember; more die in the Western world from too much food than too little.

Do not eat for a couple of hours before going to bed. If you have something to eat or a protein drink before you go to bed this will cause deep breathing during the night, will result in poor sleep and possible waking from symptoms. Sumo wrestlers intentionally have a large meal before they sleep in order to accumulate weight. The exact same process is happening to us, albeit unintentionally.

If your Control Pause is stubborn and you are experiencing difficulty increasing it even with regular physical activity then your food intake needs to be examined. For example semi-fasting or reducing meals by one per day can be very effective in increasing the Control Pause. During fasting or partial fasting dropping one meal per day will increase cortisol levels.

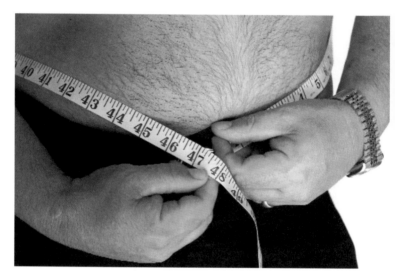

Only eat when hungry

• Reduce your protein intake

Professor Buteyko found that high protein foods such as dairy, meat and eggs increase your volume of breathing. Have you ever noticed increased symptoms or how tired you can be after eating a large dinner with meat? Professor Buteyko stated that although some people require protein, most people are better suited to a more vegetarian diet. A high protein diet is more suited to a lifestyle involving heavy work and physical activity. It is not suited to a sedentary lifestyle.

Not very inviting to the eye

- **Limit consumption of processed foods and stimulants**

Consumption of **processed foods** should be limited. In the 1930s Dr. Weston Price conducted an interesting study of traditional groups and their change to a more processed westernised diet.[1] When the Gaelic people, living on the Hebrides off the coast of Scotland, changed from their traditional diet of small sea foods and oatmeal to the modernised diet of "angel food cake, white bread and many white flour commodities, marmalade, canned vegetables, sweetened fruit juices, jams, and confections", first generation children became mouth breathers and their immunity from diseases of civilisation reduced dramatically. The traditional diets were found to provide at least four times the minimum requirement of nutrients, while modern diets did not meet the minimum requirement.

Sugar affects your adrenals which produce your body's natural source of steroid. Sugar raises blood sugar levels and causes a depletion of essential minerals such as magnesium. Interestingly, **'desserts' spelled backwards is 'stressed'.**

Little is known about the real nutritional content of **white bread**. White flour contains little nutrition and increases mucus production. To quote Dr Price's book Nutrition and Physical Degeneration: "Modern white flour has had approximately four fifths of the phosphorous and nearly all of the vitamins removed by processing, in order to produce a flour that can be shipped without becoming infested with insect life. Tests showed that white bread was unable to sustain insect life, while half a slice of whole rye bread was totally consumed by bugs." This begs the significant question: how come white bread is not good enough for bugs to eat, yet is good enough for humans to eat?

Black tea and especially **coffee** are regarded as stimulants. When Buteyko was asked if coffee was bad for you, his reply was: "Try giving it to a cat". He drew a lot of his conclusions from wild animals who instinctively know what, when and how much to eat. A person with sinus problems should avoid coffee altogether. Alternatives are herbal teas which are pleasant to drink without any side effects.

- **Eat more fresh food**

Fresh food is best. Canned food is not recommended due to the contamination of the food by aluminium packaging. Frozen vegetables, while not ideal, are a better source of prepared vegetables than canned. Best of all is **fresh fruit** and **vegetables** grown without the use of pesticides or chemical fertilisers. I remember, as a child, watching a woman in our local store who was searching for cabbages which had been attacked by slugs and other 'insects'. Her reasoning for this was that the cabbage which had been attacked by the insects had far less chemical on it. Chemicals increase your breathing rate because your body must eliminate this source of increased toxicity. Again, commercialisation and productivity take precedence over the health of the people.

Very inviting to the eye

It is beneficial to eat five portions of fresh vegetables and fruit per day, especially greens such as cabbage, broccoli, kale and kelp because these provide good sources of **magnesium and calcium.** Furthermore, vegetables do not promote the formation of mucus. Lightly cooking food and vegetables provides a richer source of nutrients and has less effect on breathing. However, the more raw the food, the less the effect it has on our breathing.

Ingredients such as **garlic, ginger, curry, onions and sea salt are beneficial**. Garlic, ginger and onions boost the immune system, thin mucus and are very helpful for people with respiratory complaints. Professor Buteyko also advocated using sea salt for cooking because it contains numerous essential minerals, thins mucus and is a natural anti-histamine.

Water

Water makes up over seventy per cent of your body and it's the single most important constituent of your diet. You consume water directly by drinking it and indirectly from your diet. You lose water each day through respiration, breathing, and elimination of waste. It is vital therefore to replenish this water loss because dehydration causes an increase of histamine levels, causing inflammation and swelling of the airway walls.

To help reduce water loss breathe only through your nose. On average we take eighteen thousand breaths over a twenty-four hour period, with this figure increasing substantially for a person who overbreathes. One of the functions of your nose is to trap moisture carried in the air on the out breath.

The second step is to reduce the group of drinks containing caffeine and alcohol. These drinks are diuretics and, while they contain water, they promote dehydration because the kidneys flush out additional water. More water leaves the body than is contained in the drink, yet many people believe that tea is a good source of water. Unfortunately it isn't and if you feel unable to reduce your tea consumption, then increase your pure water intake to counteract this loss.

The third step is to eat a diet high in water content. People who live on a water- rich diet of fruit and vegetables are free from obesity and illness and often live well in excess of one hundred years. A water-rich diet is the secret to better health and longevity. The amount of water you need depends on the type of lifestyle you lead. A person who is involved in physical activity will have a greater requirement. Likewise, it is dependent on the type of diet. If you eat a water-rich diet then the requirement to drink water is reduced.

In the medical world, there are mixed beliefs about whether thirst alone is a good indicator of the need for water. Nutritional experts suggest a daily water intake of six to eight glasses. Using this as a guide, and taking into account your individual lifestyle and diet, you can estimate individual requirements. If your lifestyle is to drink ten cups of tea a day and eat a processed food diet, then you are chronically dehydrated.

To keep your body well hydrated, adults should drink about eight glasses of water per day and make a conscious effort to maintain consistent intake.

Everyone needs water to regulate body temperature, aid respiration, transport nutrients, aid elimination of waste, provide lubrication, and give tissues their structure.

Food guidelines summary

- Eat only when you feel hungry.
- Eat until you feel satisfied. Do not continue to eat because there is food left on your plate.
- Eat fruit and vegetables each day.
- Keep hydrated- drink water.
- Eat spices, curries, ginger, garlic, onions and sea salt.

Foods to limit in quantity are:

- Milk, yoghurt, cheese, Ice cream, cream soups, chocolate.
- High protein foods such as dairy, beef, pork, chicken and eggs.
- Stimulants such as coffee, strong teas, alcohol, cocoa, soft fizzy drinks and drinking chocolate.

Chapter 7

Stressed Out

Every now and then go away,
have a little relaxation,
for when you come back to
your work your judgment will
be surer since to remain
constantly at work will cause
you to lose power of judgment.
Go some distance away
because then the work
appears smaller, and more of
it can be taken in at a glance,
and a lack of harmony or
portion is more readily seen.

--Leonardo da Vinci

Fight or Flight

Stress, a condition of the Western world, increases with life's pace. According to the famous physiologist Walter Cannon, stress activates the 'fight or flight' response. Meeting deadlines, financial pressures, the demands of rearing children, and the strain of doing well in our work add to stress levels, as do many other factors.

Long-term stress is exhausting and it is known to lead to many illnesses. Stress increases breathing, causes a loss of carbon dioxide, and resets the respiratory centre in the brain to a lower carbon dioxide level.

Stress ensures survival of the species

Stress isn't all bad news. In evolutionary terms, it's a natural reaction developed over hundreds of thousands of years to ensure the survival of our species. Invariably, stress occurs when the body undergoes chemical changes in response to environmental conditions.

Thousands of years ago, the main threat to our lives was from a rampaging wild animal. When confronted by one, we had two options to deal with it. The first was to fight the attacker, and the second was to run away from danger as quickly as possible.

In either case, our bodies were required to perform intense physical activity, so our physiology changed in a number of ways. In modern times, these physiological responses to stress are still the same and form part of that evolutionary human's 'fight or flight' response to any perceived threat.

For example:

- The breathing volume increases.
- The heart rate increases.
- Adrenaline is pumped into the system.
- The eye pupils dilate.
- Blood is diverted from internal organs to the arms and legs because these are the parts of the body most likely to be called upon to do the required fighting or fleeing.
- Diarrhoea may occur to reduce bodyweight before flight.
- The blood coagulates in case of injury.

So far, so logical… but then, the human body is an amazingly logical organism. However, in modern times our society and environment is changing at a far greater pace than the speed at which our bodies can adjust. We react to modern everyday stressors with the same reaction we would have experienced thousands of years ago when faced with a very hungry crocodile intent on seeking a handy lunch. For example, you're stuck in a traffic jam and you're absolutely desperate to get to a vital meeting on time. The body reads this situation as a threat, and the fight or flight response is activated even though there is really no need for it. Your heart rate increases; your blood is diverted to skeletal muscles and your breathing increases. By the time all these changes have taken place in your body, you are ready and primed for intense physical activity, yet you are sitting still, fuming in a snarl-up not of your making. What's the result? You are sitting still on the outside, but on the inside your body is running, and the crocodile is gaining ground....

Fight or flight while sitting still

Control Your Breathing

It's a simple physiological fact that when we get stressed, the volume of our breathing increases. You may notice this as additional sighing or mouth breathing. On the other hand, breathing may be a major physiological function but it is also under our direct control. Increased breathing feeds our stress, so it's good practice is to ensure that breathing is calm and controlled when stresses arise.

Concentrate on continuing to breathe through your nose only during stress. Play a game with yourself and try to cultivate a system of silent and still breathing. Hide your noisy breathing... if you do, the hungry and threatening lunchtime crocodile of our evolutionary days may not notice you!

Another game is this: observe other people who are under stress and listen to their breathing. Notice that they will be mouth-breathing a very large volume. Note also that this increase in breathing will further increase their stress levels. Think about the crocodile.... You're safe, but your under-stress colleague is making so much breathing noise he should make a tasty morsel!

Stress increases breathing, and increased breathing leads to a loss of residual carbon dioxide in the blood. This loss causes arterial vessels and capillaries to constrict. The constriction reduces blood flow to the brain. In addition, less oxygen is delivered due to the Bohr effect. Both factors lead to an increase in the excitability of brain cells, thereby increasing stress.

Big breathers are naturally more stressed than correct volume healthy breathers. A person with a high control pause will be a lot more relaxed and calm than a person with a lower control pause. Invariably, people who experience panic or hyperventilation attacks are big breathers.

People who exercise are more relaxed

Primarily, the body changes to help us when we are stressed. The body is programmed for physical activity when we are stressed. How do you deal with this? Your body is ready to fight or flee, so release this activation of your system by taking a walk or a jog or whatever exercise appeals to you. If you're stuck in that traffic jam or another stressful situation and you're not able to remove yourself from your environment, then control your breathing at the time, but later that day make sure you participate in a physical activity.

People who exercise regularly are calmer and more productive than their colleagues. Exercise enables quicker recovery from stress. Chemicals are released in your body during the 'fight or flight' response but they are removed quicker during exercise and therefore the body's systems can return to their normal operating rate.

Exercise also promotes the release of pent-up negative energy, enhances self-esteem and is a useful way to recharge your batteries by escaping from work and other commitments for a while. You win, and the crocodile goes hungry!

A great way to start the day.

Conclusion

**"Nature does not hurry,
yet everything is
accomplished."**

- Lao Tzu

Correct breathing volume is a holistic approach and is probably the single most positive influence you can have on your health during your lifetime. Bearing this in mind, it should be approached with good intent, discipline and determination.

Your over-riding goal is to reduce the volume of air that passes through your lungs to more correct physiological levels. You know you are achieving this when you begin to feel better and when your control pause is increasing.

The two steps to correct breathing:

· Increased observation of breathing. Breathing is a twenty-four hour activity, so it is important to observe it periodically throughout the day. Pay attention to your breathing and ask yourself if it is gentle, calm, regular, silent and as still as if you are not breathing, or if it's noisy, irregular, uneven, raspy and loud. If your breathing sounds like the latter, then it's time to take steps to change it.

Activities such as eating, sleeping, stress, and physical activity affect breathing. By increasing your own awareness, you will notice many factors which increase your breathing. This may be your tendency to eat a huge meal, your stress levels at work, or it may be any one of other features of modern civilisation.

• It will require considerable attention to reverse a bad habit which you have been unintentionally and unwittingly practising for all your life. Regular practice of breathing exercises is necessary to retrain the body to accept a reduced and healthier volume of breathing. It also helps you understand what it means exactly to breathe in a calm, gentle and regular manner.

For the first couple of months it is important to set aside time to perform breathing exercises. The reason for this is that you will not make progress if all your exercises are completed while reading a book, watching TV or driving because your concentration will be divided between doing the exercises and whatever else you're doing at the time. However, following a number of months' practice, you will be entirely familiar with the concept of reduced breathing and so will be able to apply it in almost any place or situation.

Close your mouth for perfect health

By reading this book, you have taken the first step towards improving your health forever. It will take time so be patient; it will take determination so persevere; it will take observation so be aware.

Breathing is the only function of critical importance over which we can exercise control. We cannot voluntarily increase oxygen and blood flow to tissues and organs; we cannot voluntarily reduce our blood pressure; we cannot voluntarily order the airways to open, but we can influence all these vital functions by addressing an incorrect breathing pattern. In my opinion it is now time to educate the Western world to the detrimental effects of overbreathing.

In this book, I have tried to encourage you to become more aware of your breathing. Normally we do not have to remember to breathe in and out; it happens naturally. So it is probable that this will be the first time in your life that you will be so observant of and aware of your breathing. At the same time however, it is possible to exercise a measure of control over our breathing: we can change the volume, and we can also influence the rate, within certain parameters.

You now have the tools to take control of your health naturally, safely and effectively. Start applying them. Do what you can to help your condition. It is your life and your health, and the power rests within you.

I want to close by wishing you every success in using this approach to help you and your children with breath retraining, and I hope that this book will help as many people as possible to gain control of their health with minimal or no medication.

Naturally.

"To tell the truth is not only a responsibility to yourself and others. It is an honour, a duty and your legacy to the generations to come. It is part of their rightful inheritance."

- Unknown

Appendix One

Mater Hospital Trials 1995

Summary of blind randomised trial at the Mater Hospital, Brisbane, 1995.
Duration: January to April 1995
Trial sample: 39 people

The purpose of the trial was to evaluate the therapeutic benefits of the Buteyko Breathing Method as a treatment for asthma. The trial was funded by a grant from the Australian Association of Asthma Foundations and conducted by Professor Charles Mitchell.

Trial Results

Exacerbation of symptoms

During the three months of the study, three subjects from each group were admitted to hospital. In addition, six subjects from the Buteyko Method group and seven subjects from the control group received short courses of oral steroids. An approximate number of severe chronic asthmatics were involved in both groups.

Medication usage after three months

Buteyko Group	
Average reduction in reliever use:	90%
Average reduction in steroid use:	49%
Daily symptom score:	71% improvement

Control Group	
Average reduction in reliever use:	14.78%
Average reduction in steroid use:	0%
Daily symptom score:	14% improvement

Conclusions

The Buteyko Breathing group experienced a significant reduction in the need for reliever medication and steroids, along with a greater improvement in quality of life.

The control group showed little change in medication and quality of life despite being taught the conventional breathing exercises that continue to be the mainstay of treatment in hospitals and clinics.

A headline from an article published in Australian Doctor read "Doctors gasp at Buteyko success". Dr Simon Bowler, a respiratory physician at Mater Hospital in Brisbane was quoted as saying "we were surprised at the results, as we didn't expect any significant changes." [1]

Those who reduced their breathing volume the most were able to reduce their symptoms - and therefore their medication - the most. In addition, no contraindications or dangers were cited throughout the trials or during the reviews afterwards.

Buteyko's theory is that because hyperventilation causes asthma, a reduction in overbreathing results in a reduction of asthma severity and therefore the need for medication. This was indeed proven by the trials.

Appendix Two

Gisborne Hospital Trials 2003

A blind randomised trial involving 38 people aged between 18 and 70 with asthma was conducted at Gisborne Hospital, New Zealand under the guidance of Dr Patrick McHugh.

Buteyko Group at six months
50% reduction of inhaled steroid
85% reduction of bronchodilator (reliever)

Control group at six months
0% change of inhaled steroid
37% reduction of bronchodilator (reliever)

There were no adverse events recorded in either group.

Conclusion of trial as published in The New Zealand Medical Journal. Vol 116. No 1187:

"BBT (Buteyko Breathing Technique) is a safe and efficacious asthma management technique.

BBT has clinical and potential pharmo-economic benefits that merit further study".

Appendix Three

During a debate in the British House of Commons, Westminster, London, on June 25th, 2000, Mrs. **Anne Campbell (Cambridge)** commented as follows:

"It is time we admitted that the current treatments appear to be making us worse, not better, and I want to take a look at the possible causes and treatment of asthma. I shall describe the work done by a Russian doctor, Konstantin Buteyko, in the 1960s; it attempted to explain why people get asthma, and offered a management regime for the disease. Buteyko blames hyperventilation for a number of civilisation-induced diseases. We all hyperventilate at times of stress.

There are some well-documented cases of people who have been helped by the technique. I understand that Jonathan Aitken, when he was Chief Secretary to the Treasury, received treatment from a Buteyko practitioner in London. His asthma was moderately severe, but over a course of consultations and home visits he made a dramatic recovery. A newspaper article quoted him as saying: 'I have tried plenty of treatments, but this is the only one that has really worked. I think it is a remarkable one that could help many people.'

Con Barrell, a member of the New Zealand All-Black team, said after his treatment: 'I sleep better, my pulse rate has dropped 10-12 beats on a regular basis and I feel well. This has been a big help to me as a professional and personally. I recommend asthmatics try it-things can only get better.'

As someone who has suffered from asthma for 40 years and whose condition would have been previously described as moderate, I have given the Buteyko technique a try myself.

What I really regret is that no one told me about the method before. This year I have not suffered from any hay fever, except for a very occasional sneeze, and I wish that someone had told me about the technique some time ago. Alone, I could have saved the National Health Service hundred pounds worth of medication and myself a lot of needless discomfort. However, the Minister, whom I am happy to welcome to the Front Bench, will be less impressed by anecdote than by medical trials. Unfortunately, there is little evidence to quote so far."

Later during the same debate, the same speaker had this to contribute:
"In referring to the effectiveness of the Buteyko

method, the National Asthma Campaign remarks on its website: 'Lack of published research makes it difficult to reach a conclusion on its effectiveness.'

Buteyko himself conducted a trial in Russia, but the results were considered to be too good, and were not believed for many years.

In December 1998 a paper by Bowler, Green and Mitchell was published in *Alternative Medicine*, in Australia. The paper was called *Buteyko breathing techniques in asthma: a blinded randomised trial*. The trial compared the effect of the Buteyko breathing technique with a control group in thirty-nine subjects with asthma. The control group was given instruction in general asthma education, relaxation techniques and abdominal breathing exercises. The experimenters looked at medication use, peak flow and quality of life, among other factors.

After three months, the subjects assigned to the Buteyko group had reduced their reliever medication by 904 micrograms, whereas the control group had a reduction of 57 micrograms - a highly significant result at the 0.2 per cent level of significance. There was also a reduction in inhaled steroid use by the Buteyko subjects, although the sample sizes were too small for that to be statistically significant.

Similarly and more importantly, perhaps from my point of view, there was a trend towards greater improvement in the mean quality of life scores of the

Buteyko group. I certainly think that if someone can have uninterrupted sleep, feel better and have more energy, it is worth a great deal to that individual.

I very much hope that as a result of this adjournment debate, my Honourable Friend will ask the Chief Medical Officer to examine the available evidence.

Let me stress that the technique that I have described does not constitute alternative medicine - a term normally used to describe techniques that sometimes succeed, although no-one can quite work out why. The Buteyko technique was derived from research carried out by Konstantin Buteyko, who devised a programme from his theory. The fact that it has worked for me, as well as for many others, must suggest that at the very least it is worth investigating further. I hope that the Minister will respond positively to that suggestion.

Appendix Four

Konstantin Pavlovich Buteyko

Konstantin Pavlovich Buteyko was born near Kiev in the Ukraine on January 27th, 1923. This simple yet extraordinary man devoted his life to studying the human organism and made one of the most profound discoveries in the history of medicine.

Buteyko commenced his medical training in Russia in 1946 at the First Medical Institute of Moscow. Part of one of his practical assignments involved monitoring the breathing of terminally ill patients prior to death. After hundreds of hours spent observing and recording breathing patterns, he was able to predict with accuracy, often to the minute, the time of death of each patient. Each patient's breathing increased as their condition deteriorated and as they approached death.

While at University Buteyko was diagnosed as suffering from malignant hypertension, a fatal form of blood pressure which gave him life expectancy of just 12 months. Under the guidance of his tutors Buteyko researched his illness in depth although it seemed that there was very little that he could do to reverse it.

On October 7th,1952 after majoring in clinical therapy, he began to wonder whether the cause of his condition, which was going from bad to worse, might be his deep breathing. He checked this by reducing his breathing. Within minutes his headache, the pain in his right kidney and his heartache ceased. To confirm his discovery, he took five deep breaths and the pain returned. He again reversed his deep breathing and the pain disappeared.

He did not appreciate it at the time, but this was one of the greatest, although as yet largely unacknowledged, medical discoveries of the twentieth century. Buteyko established that breathing, so vital in sustaining life, can be not alone the cure but also, amazingly, the cause of so many of diseases of civilisation.

Buteyko measured the breathing patterns of patients suffering from asthma, but he also included in his research sufferers from other ailments and found in many cases that they too hyperventilated between attacks. After many years research, he went on to work on the theoretical aspects of his discovery at the Central and Lenin Medical Libraries. He devised a programme to measure breathing and also a method of reconditioning patients' breathing to normal levels.

This involved:

1. Switching from mouth breathing to nasal breathing.

2. Relaxation of the diaphragm until an air shortage is felt.

3. Small lifestyle changes are necessary to assist with this, thus commencing the road to full recovery.

Buteyko received a cold reception from the medical establishment at the time. In order to have his discovery accepted he commenced clinical research on a mixed group of two hundred people - some sick and some healthy, in 1959. On January 11th, 1960 he demonstrated to the Scientific Forum at the Institute the correlation between depth of breathing, carbon dioxide levels in the body and state of health.

However, for many of his colleagues Dr. Buteyko offered too great a challenge to many of the theories upon which medicine was based. Surely illness, for which the conventional medical remedy was surgery and/or extensive medication, could not be dealt with simply by a change in breathing. Yet this was exactly what Buteyko demonstrated. And while not receiving outright acceptance, Buteyko did gain the temporary support of Professor Meshalkin, the chairman of the Forum, in enabling the research to continue.

In the years that followed, Buteyko continued his research, assisted by a team of two hundred qualified medical personnel and using the most up to date technology. By 1967 over one thousand patients with asthma, and other illnesses, had recovered from their conditions using his methods.

In April 1980, following trials in Leningrad and at the First Moscow Institute of Pediatric Diseases, the Buteyko Breathing Method was officially acknowledged as having a one hundred per cent success rate. This research was directed by the Soviet Ministry's Committee for Science and Technology.

The USSR Committee on Inventions and Discoveries formally acknowledged Buteyko's discovery in 1983 and issued the patent entitled "The method of treatment of hypocapnia", (Authors certificate No. 1067640 issued on September 15th, 1983). Interestingly, the date of the discovery as listed in the document was backdated to January 29th, 1962. His discovery was officially recognised twenty years after it had been made.

Over two hundred medical professionals teach this therapy at present from centres located in major towns throughout Russia. Buteyko wrote over fifty scientific publications detailing the relationship between respiration and carbon dioxide and at least five Ph.D. dissertations were written by his colleagues. The basis of the Buteyko Clinic Method detailing the relationship between carbon dioxide and breath holding-time forms part of medical curriculum at Universities.

I was very fortunate to meet and speak with Professor Buteyko during March 2002 at the Buteyko Clinic of Moscow. At the time of meeting, his health was failing due to a very serious car accident in which he had been involved ten years previously. Although he visited the clinic regularly, he had retired at that time and instead devoted his mind to matters of a more spiritual nature.

On Friday, May 2nd 2003 at 4.05 p.m. (Moscow time), Professor Buteyko parted from this world with some very deep inspirations. His death came as quite a shock to the many people around the world who had experienced excellent health as a result of his life's work. His wish was to be buried in the country of his birth, the Ukraine. His resting place is in Feodosia in the Crimea, Ukraine.

His memory will live on and I feel will grow in momentum as more and more people hear about his discovery.

In 1990 the Buteyko Breathing Method was brought outside Russia to Australia by Sasha Stalmatski. In 1995 Stalmatski brought this method to the UK and, for a number of years, it has been practised at the famous Hale Clinic (opened in 1988 by Prince Charles).

Buteyko's Method challenges the belief that overbreathing is beneficial and also uncovers many causes of illness unexplained by modern medicine. It seems extraordinary that modern medicine, with all its research and resources, human, technical and scientific, has continually failed to verify the link between overbreathing and various medical conditions, notably asthma.

The efforts which Buteyko had to make to have his discovery recognised also seem to indicate an unwillingness on the part of the medical community to accept discoveries not pharmaceutically based - in part perhaps because they challenge long standing and sincerely held beliefs.

My own belief is that the Buteyko clinic method will in time gain full acceptance from the medical community, although it may take some years. The quicker this can be accomplished, the greater the contribution that Buteyko's discovery will make to the health of mankind.

Appendix Five

Useful contact information

Asthma Care Ireland incorporating Buteyko Breathing Clinic

Dublin, Cork, Limerick, Galway, Sligo and Athlone
Freefone 1800 931 935 for a free information pack
E-mail: info@asthmacare.ie
Website: http://www.asthmacare.ie

Asthma Care Ireland provide Buteyko Clinic workshops for people with respiratory disorders and other complaints.

* Workshops conducted by Buteyko Breathing Clinic are taught according to the standards and method of the Buteyko Clinic of Moscow.

References

Chapter two:
1) J Indian Soc Pedod Prev Dent. 1998 Sep;16(3):72-83 A comparative study of effects of mouth breathing and normal breathing on gingival health in children (Gulati MS, Grewal N, Kaur A.)

Chapter four:
1) Bed-wetters could breathe easier. July, 30th, 2003, 19:00, New Scientist.

Chapter six:
1) Dr Weston Price Nutrition and physical degeneration

Appendix One
1) Australian Doctor 7 April 1995.

Additional References
1) Breathing Free by Teresa Hale
2) Buteyko Support Group worldwide organised by Peter Kolb of Australia
3) Freedom From Asthma by Alexander Stalmatski
4) What science and Professor Buteyko teach us about breathing by Artour Rakhimov Ph.D.
5) Personal correspondence with Dr Andrey Novozhilov
6) Breathe Well, Be Well by Robert Fried Ph.D.
7) Every Breath You Take by Dr. Paul J. Ameisen
8) Hyperventilation Syndrome by Dinah Bradley
9) The Tao of Natural Breathing by Dennis Lewis
10) Asthma Free Naturally by Patrick McKeown.

Many Acknowledgments
for this little book

Special thanks to editor Angela Doyle and paper tigers for their undivided attention and timeliness.

I am extremely grateful to Liam and Anne Maher and family for their continued support and encouragement. I am also deeply thankful to Bill Power for his early editing of the manuscript, his very helpful insights, his sense of humour and feedback.

Special thanks to Kevin Kelly, author of two self help Books; How When You Don't Know How, and Life a Trip Towards Trust. Kevin provided me with an accurate expectation of the trials and tribulations of writing this book, from the first written word to final completion.

To those people who willingly gave up their time to be interviewed on RTE and TV3 and the Irish media, thank you so much for helping to create greater awareness of this therapy. A special thanks to Anthony Garvey, Richard and Peter Moran, Yvonne and Lorcan Cooke, Elizabeth Mullins, Shane Fitzgibbon, Sue Emerson, Liam Lawlor (not the politician), Maura Coyle, Aoife Quinn, Anne Wilson and Jean McConnell.

Thank you Global Solutions for all your help and professionalism regarding cover design and illustrations throughout. Thank you iSupply for your careful attention with typesetting.

Credit for the various photographs go to Daniel Martinez for city at speed p.50, George G. Chiodo for afternoon working in country p.86, Sam Choi, Hong Kong for vegetable stall p.104 and exercise in Hong Hong p.114, all other photos are from istockphoto.com.
Special thanks to Dr Andrey Novozhilov and Luidmilla Buteyko, my teachers, and to the greatest scientist of all time, the late Professor Konstantin Buteyko. Thank you for your undivided attention and for providing humanity with its greatest discovery to date.

To Sinead, the balance in my life, my partner and soul mate, thank you.
Finally, I would like to express my love and gratitude to my mother, father and brothers, without whom this book would not exist.

A special hello to P.J Wheeler who inspired the photograph on p100.

Diary of Progress

Date														
Time														
Pulse														
CP														
RB 5 min														
Cp														
Rb 5 min														
CP														
RB 5 min														
Cp														
Rb 5 min														
CP														
Pulse														

CP means Control Pause. **RB 5 min** means reduced breathing for five minutes.

Date																		
Time																		
Pulse																		
CP																		
RB 5 min																		
Cp																		
Rb 5 min																		
CP																		
RB 5 min																		
Cp																		
Rb 5 min																		
CP																		
Pulse																		

CP means Control Pause, **RB 5 min** means reduced breathing for five minutes. Rest for one minute before taking **CP.**

Diary of Progress

(Steps page1)

Date																			
Time																			
CP																			
Steps																			
Steps																			
Steps																			
CP																			
Steps																			
Steps																			
Steps																			
CP																			

CP means Control Pause.

Diary of Progress

(Steps page 2)

Date																
Time																
CP																
Steps																
Steps																
Steps																
CP																
Steps																
Steps																
Steps																
CP																

CP means Control Pause.